THE LION KING

MUSIC FROM THE MOTION PICTURE SOUNDTRACK

T0082026

ISBN 978-1-5400-6582-7

Visit Hal Leonard Online at
www.halleonard.com

Contact us:
Hal Leonard
7777 West Bluemound Road
Milwaukee, WI 53213
Email: info@halleonard.com

In Europe, contact:
Hal Leonard Europe Limited
42 Wigmore Street
Marylebone, London, W1U 2RN
Email: info@halleonardeurope.com

In Australia, contact:
Hal Leonard Australia Pty. Ltd.
4 Lentara Court
Cheltenham, Victoria, 3192 Australia
Email: info@halleonard.com.au

Circle of Life

Music by Elton John
Lyrics by Tim Rice

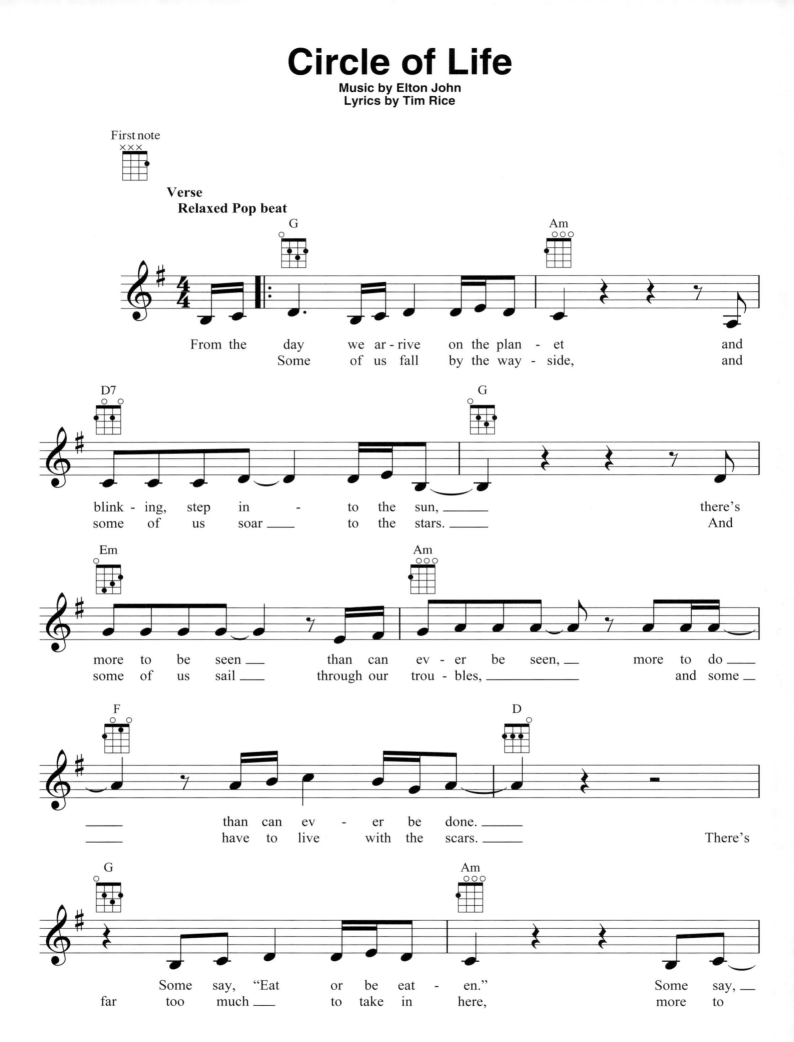

"Live and let live." ____ But
find than can ev - er be found. ____ But the

all are a - greed __ as they join the stam - pede, __ you should
sun roll - ing high __ through the sap - phi - re sky __ keeps great and

nev - er take more __ than you give _____ in the cir - cle of life. __
small on the end - less __ round _____ in the cir - cle of life. __

Chorus

____ } It's the wheel of for - tune.

It's the leap of faith. ____ It's the band of __ hope __

____ 'til we find ____ our __ place _____

3

on the path un-wind - ing   in the cir-

To Coda ⊕

1.

- cle, _____   the cir - cle of life. _____

D.S. al Coda

2.

the cir - cle of life! _____

⊕ **Coda**

the cir - cle of life. _____

Outro

On the path un-wind - ing   in the cir - cle, _____

the cir - cle of life. _____

I Just Can't Wait to Be King

Music by Elton John
Lyrics by Tim Rice

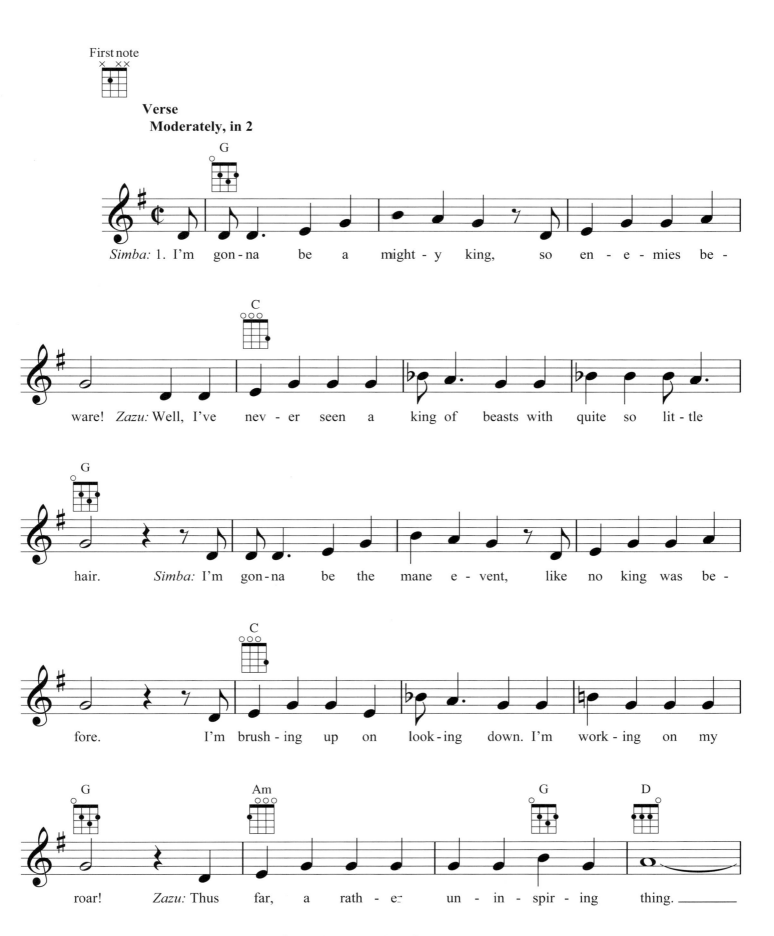

Simba: Oh, I just can't _____ wait to be

king!

Zazu (Spoken:)
You've rather a long way to go, young master! If you think... _Simba:_ No one say - ing

Chorus

Zazu (Spoken:) Now, when _I said that, I..._ _What I_

"do this," no one say - ing "be there,"

meant was that the... _But what you don't realize..._

no one say - ing "stop that," no one say - ing

Now see here!

"see here." _____ Free to run a - round all _____

Well, that's definitely out.

day, free to do it all my _____

way!

(Quasi spoken:)

Zazu: 2. I

Verse

think it's time that you and I ar - ranged a heart - to -

heart. *Simba:* Kings don't need ad - vice from lit - tle

(Sung:)

horn - bills, for a start. *Zazu:* If this is where the

(Quasi spoken:)

mon - ar - chy is head - ed, count me out! Out of

ser - vice, out of Af - ri - ca ___ I would - n't hang a -

hear it in the herd and on ____ the wing. _____ It's

gon - na be King Sim - ba's fin - est fling. *Simba:* Oh, I

just can't ____ wait to be king. Oh, I

just can't ____ wait to be king. Oh, I

Outro

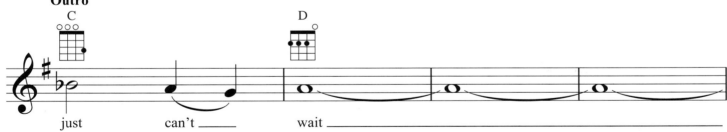

just can't ____ wait _____

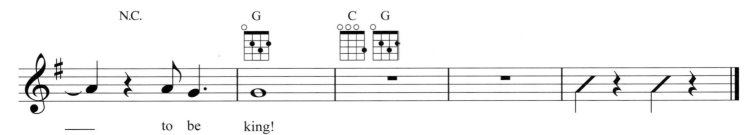

____ to be king!

Be Prepared

(2019)

Music by Elton John
Lyrics by Tim Rice

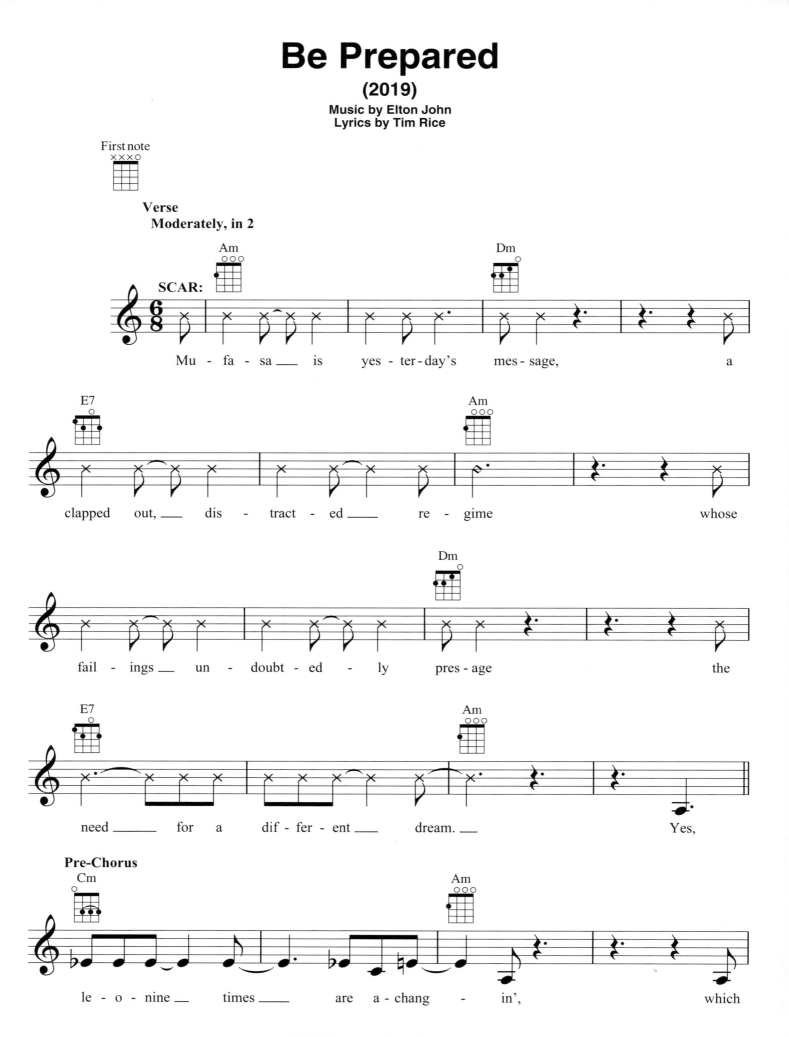

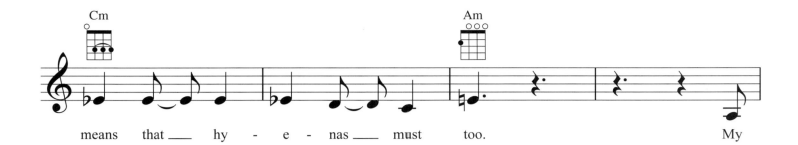

means that ___ hy - e - nas ___ must too. My

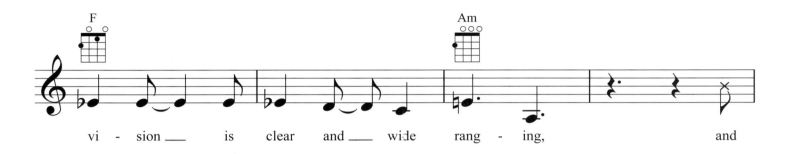

vi - sion ___ is clear and ___ wide rang - ing, and

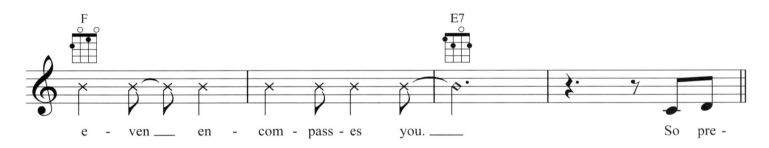

e - ven ___ en - com - pass - es you. ___ So pre -

Chorus

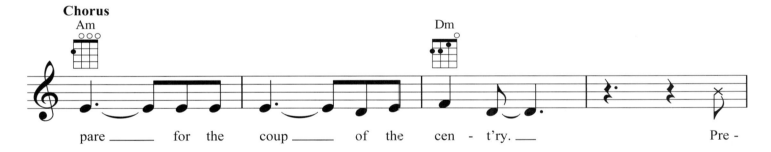

pare ___ for the coup ___ of the cen - t'ry. ___ Pre -

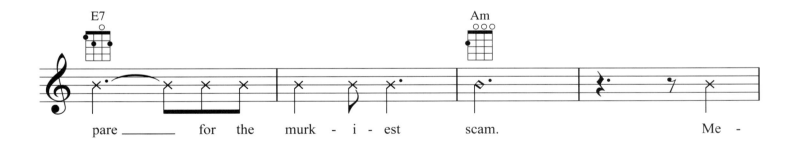

pare ___ for the murk - i - est scam. Me -

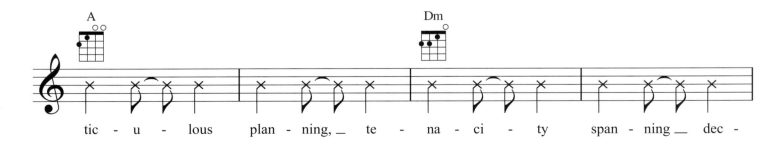

tic - u - lous plan - ning, ___ te - na - ci - ty span - ning ___ dec -

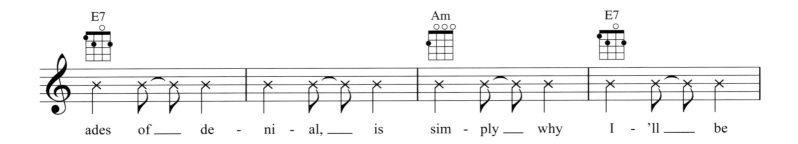

ades of ___ de - ni - al, ___ is sim - ply ___ why I - 'll ___ be

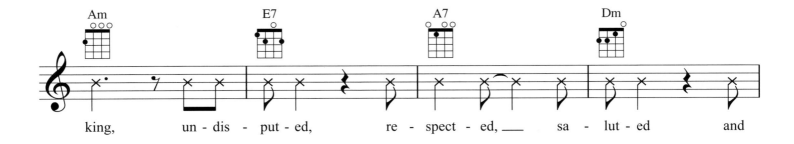

king, un - dis - put - ed, re - spect - ed, ___ sa - lut - ed and

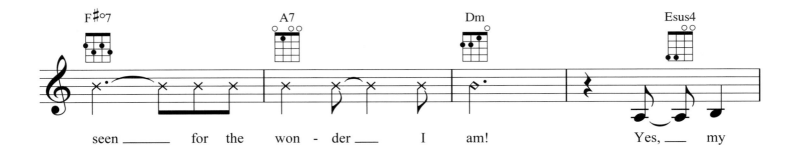

seen _____ for the won - der ___ I am! Yes, ___ my

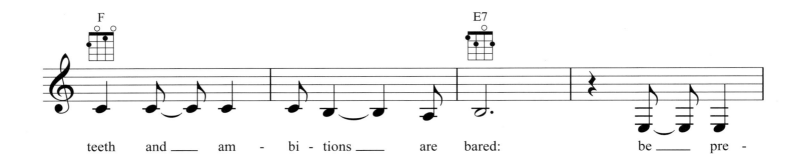

teeth and ___ am - bi - tions ___ are bared: be ___ pre -

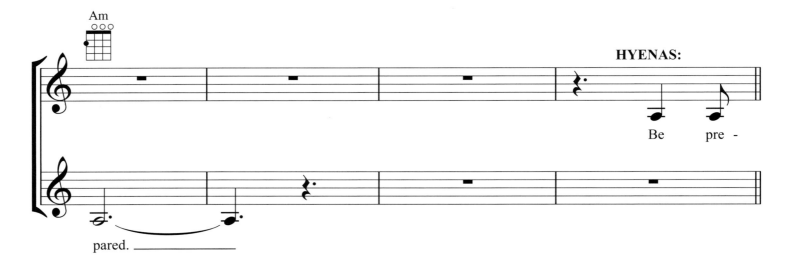

HYENAS:

Be pre -

pared. _____

The Lion Sleeps Tonight

New Lyrics and Revised Music by George David Weiss, Hugo Peretti and Luigi Creatore

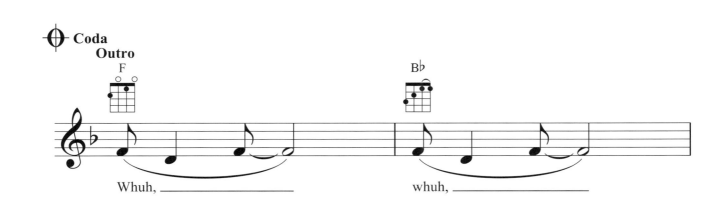

Whuh, _____ whuh, _____

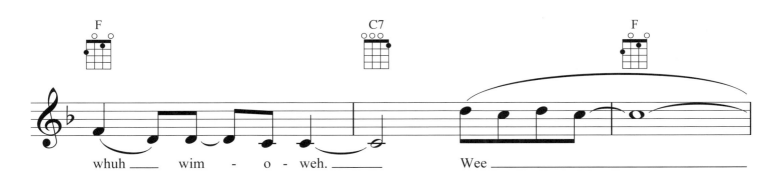

whuh _____ wim - o - weh. _____ Wee _____

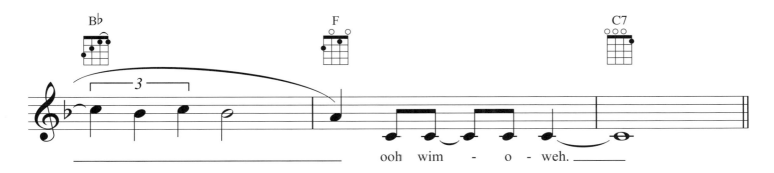

_____ ooh wim - o - weh. _____

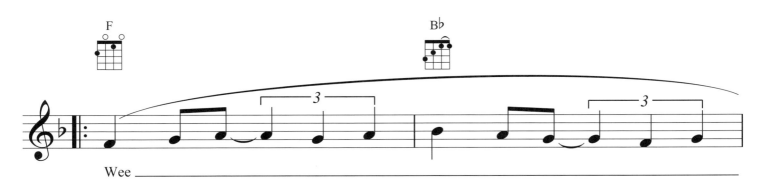

Wee _____

_____ ooh wim - o - weh. _____

Repeat and fade

Hakuna Matata

Music by Elton John
Lyris by Tim Rice

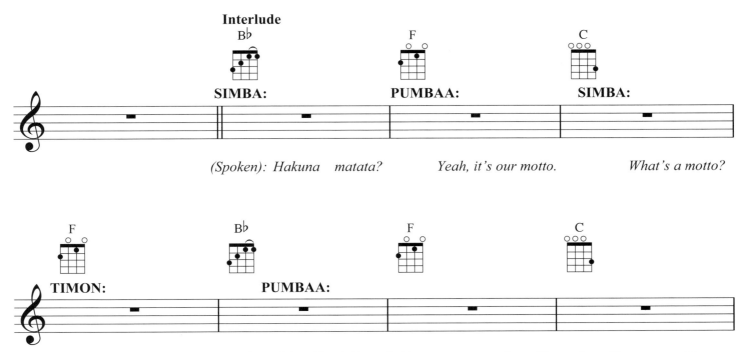

Interlude

SIMBA: PUMBAA: SIMBA:

(Spoken): Hakuna matata?   *Yeah, it's our motto.*   *What's a motto?*

TIMON: PUMBAA:

Nothin'! What's - a - motto with you?!   *Nice! Boom! Those two words will solve all your problems.*

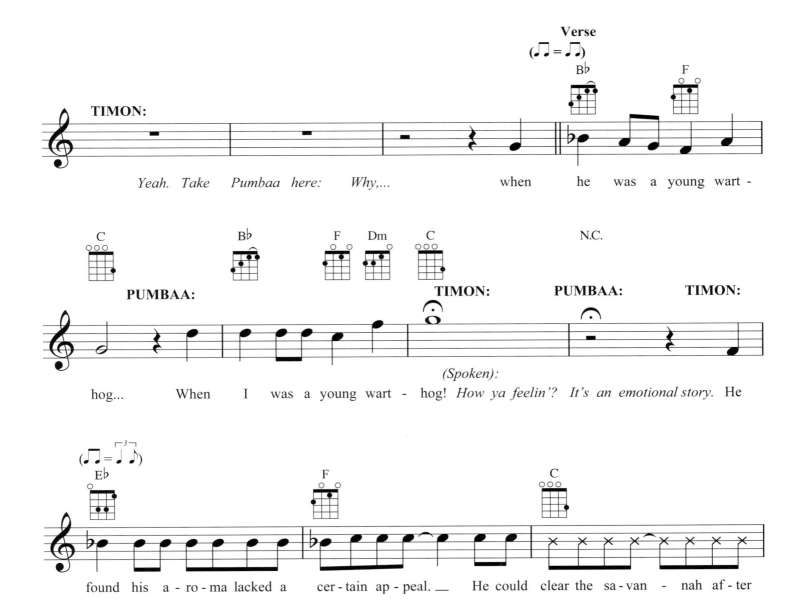

Verse

TIMON:

Yeah. Take Pumbaa here: *Why,...*   when   he   was   a   young   wart -

PUMBAA: TIMON: PUMBAA: TIMON:

hog...   When   I   was   a   young   wart -   hog!   *How ya feelin'?*   *(Spoken):* *It's an emotional story.*   He

found   his   a - ro - ma   lacked   a   cer - tain ap - peal.   He   could   clear   the   sa - van - nah   af - ter

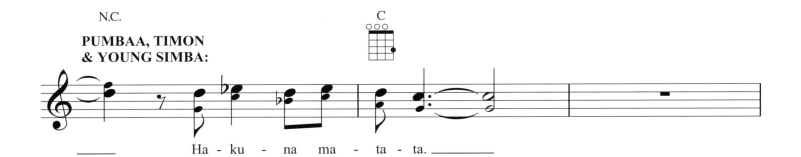

Ha - ku - na ma - ta - ta. _____

Bridge

ALL:

Ha - ku - na ma - ta - ta. Ha-

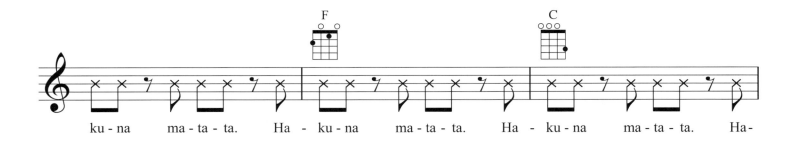

ku - na ma - ta - ta. Ha - ku - na ma - ta - ta. Ha - ku - na ma - ta - ta. Ha-

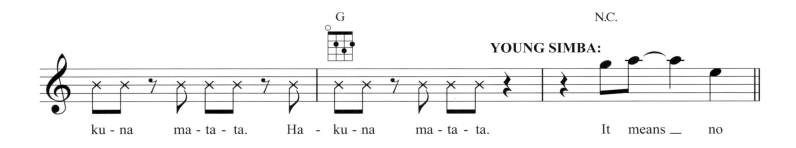

YOUNG SIMBA:

ku - na ma - ta - ta. Ha - ku - na ma - ta - ta. It means ___ no

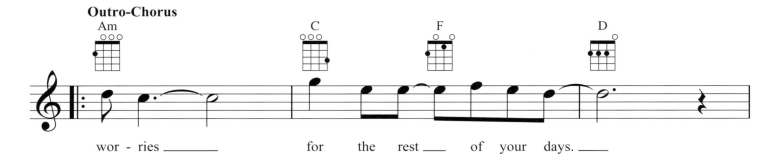

Outro-Chorus

wor - ries _____ for the rest ___ of your days. ___

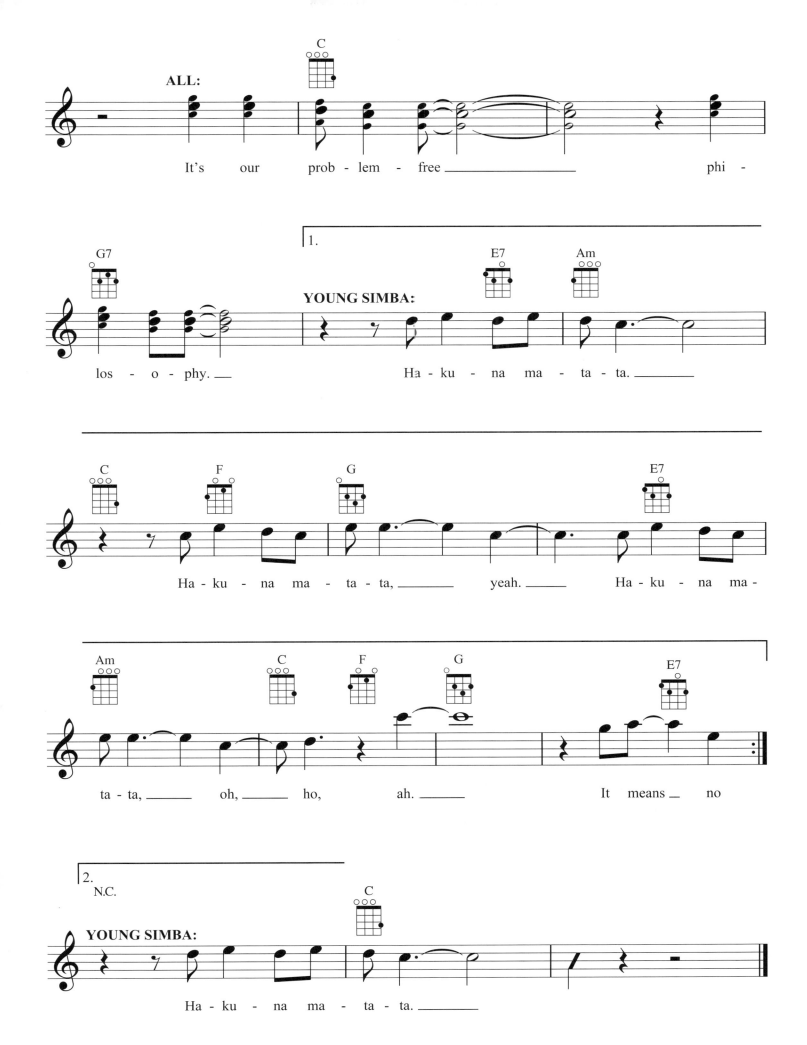

Can You Feel the Love Tonight

Music by Elton John
Lyrics by Tim Rice

Verse
Moderately slow, in 2

1. There's a calm surrender to the rush of day,
2. There's a time for ev-'ry-one, if they on-ly learn

when the heat of the roll-ing world can be turned a-way.
that the twist-ing ka-lei-do-scope moves us all in turn.

An en-chant-ed mo-ment, and it sees me through.
There's a rhyme and rea-son to the wild out-doors

It's e-nough for this rest-less war-rior just to be with you.
when the heart of this star-crossed voy-ag-er beats in time with yours.

And

Chorus

can you feel the love to-night?
can you feel the love to-night,

Spirit

Written by Timothy McKenzie, Ilya Salmanzadeh and Beyoncé

Bridge

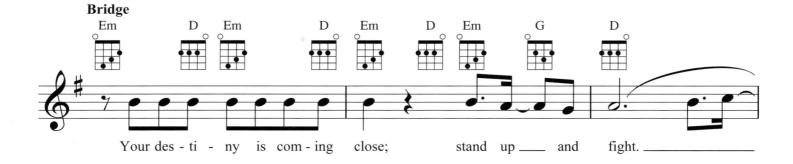

Your des - ti - ny is com - ing close; stand up ___ and fight. ___

___ So, go ___ in - to that far - off ___ land ___ and be ___

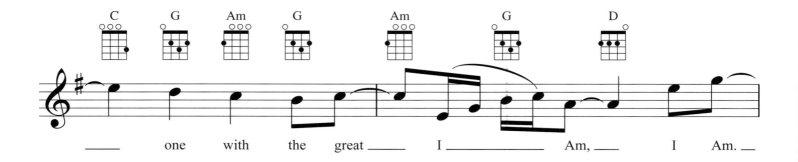

___ one with the great ___ I ___ Am, ___ I Am. ___

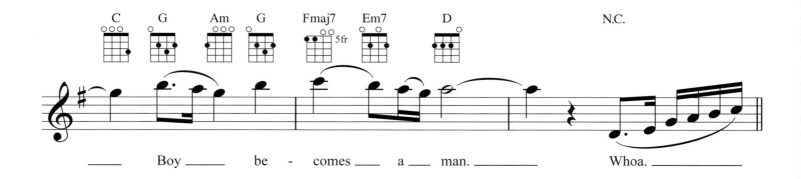

___ Boy ___ be - comes ___ a ___ man. ___ Whoa. ___

Chorus

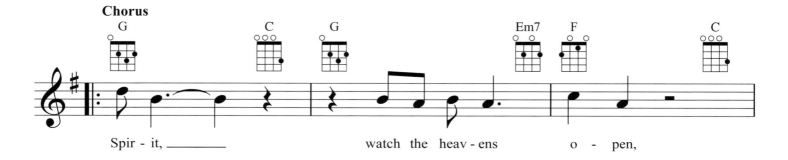

Spir - it, ___ watch the heav - ens o - pen,

yeah. _____ Spir - it, _____ can you hear it call - ing?

Yeah. _____ **Outro** Your des - ti - ny is com - ing close;

stand up ____ and fight. _____ So, go ____

____ in - to that far - off _____ land ____ and be ____

____ one with the great _____ I _____ Am. _____

Never Too Late

Music by Elton John
Lyrics by Tim Rice

get at least some, ___ if not all _____ of it back. _____ I
have to be no - ticed, don't have _____ to be crowned. __ I

thought I was hap - py, and some - times I was, ___ but
did what I've done, ___ and I don't try to hide. ___ I

sad - ness is just _____ as im - por - tant be - cause, got to car -
lost man - y things, __ but nev - er my pride. It's nev -

- ry the weight and hope it's nev - er too late. __
- er too late, I know, it's nev - er too late. __

Chorus

___ } Nev - er too late to fight the fight.

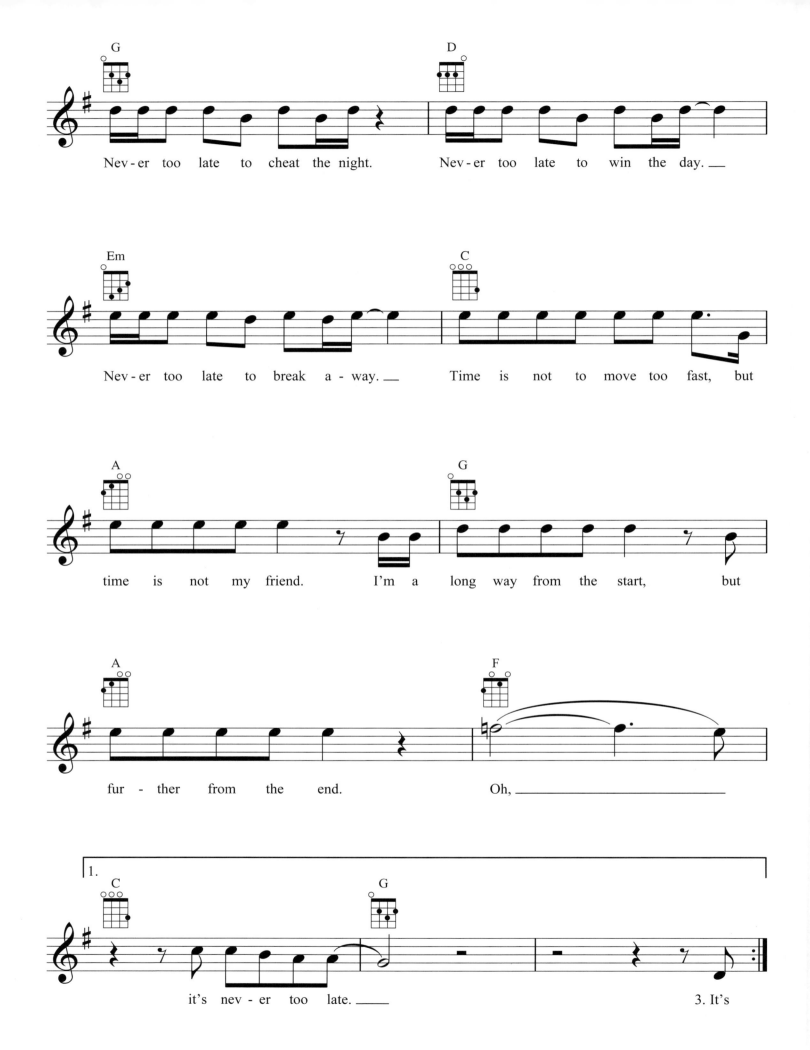

Nev-er too late to cheat the night. Nev-er too late to win the day. ___

Nev-er too late to break a-way. ___ Time is not to move too fast, but

time is not my friend. I'm a long way from the start, but

fur-ther from the end. Oh, ___

1.

it's nev-er too late. ___ 3. It's

it's nev-er too late. ____ *(Vocal ad lib.)*

Bridge

used to say, "I don't have time, I'm sleep-ing to-night." __ A

day do-in' noth-in' is do-in' it right. __ No

hur-ry, no hur-ry, it takes as long as it takes. You

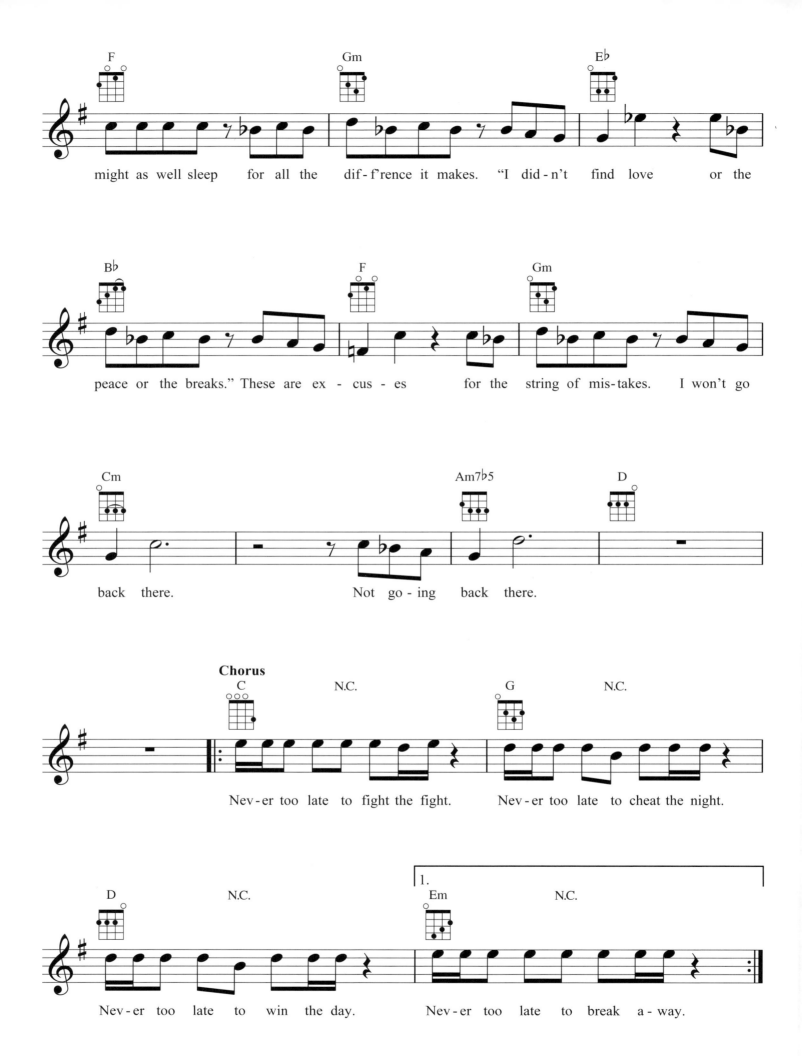

might as well sleep   for all the   dif-f'rence it makes.   "I did-n't   find   love   or the

peace or the breaks." These are ex - cus - es   for the   string of mis-takes.   I won't go

back   there.   Not go - ing   back   there.

Chorus

Nev - er too late to fight the fight.   Nev - er too late to cheat the night.

1.

Nev - er too late to win the day.   Nev - er too late to break a - way.

Nev-er too late to break a-way. Time is not to move too fast, but time is not my friend. I'm a

long way from the start, but fur-ther from the end. ___ Oh, _____

Outro

it's nev - er too late. _____ It's nev - er too late. ___

___ Oh! It's nev - er too late. ___

It's nev-er too late. ___ It's nev-er too late. ___

He Lives in You

Lyrics and Music by Mark Mancina, Jay Rifkin and Lebohang Morake

Ne - zwi.   E - li - no - yi - ko ____ lwe nt - sa - na.

Liya - phen - du - la,   Whoa, ___ ma - me - la. ____

U - bu - kho - si bo kho - kho. ___   Yi -

Pre-Chorus

- ma. ___   A - ku - kho bun - zi - ma. _____

Yi - va la - ma - zwi ___ u - ha - le ____ e them -

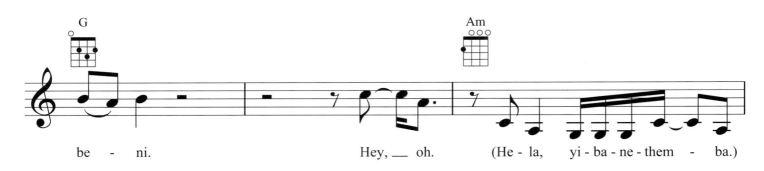

be - ni.   Hey, ___ oh.   (He - la, yi - ba - ne - them - ba.)

(He - la, yi - ba - ne - them - ba.) (He - la, yi - ba - ne - them - ba.) U - phi - la
(He - la, hey, ma - me - la.)

Chorus

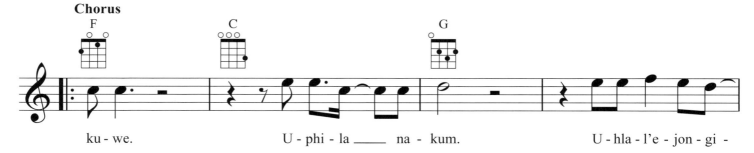

ku - we.   U - phi - la _____ na - kum.   U - hla - l'e - jon - gi -

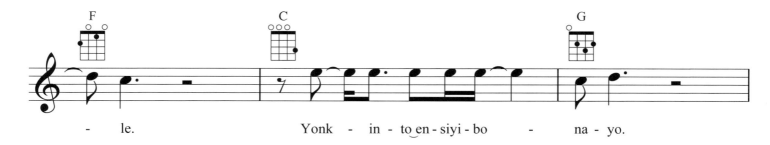

- le.   Yonk - in - to en - siyi - bo - na - yo.

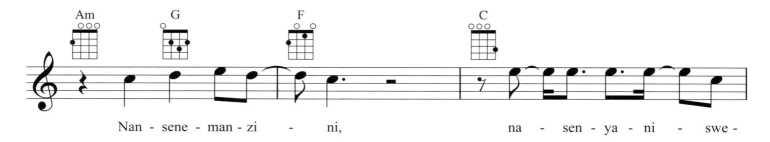

Nan - sene - man - zi - ni,   na - sen - ya - ni - swe -

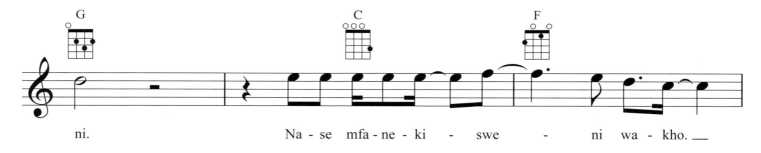

ni.   Na - se mfa - ne - ki - swe - ni wa - kho. _____

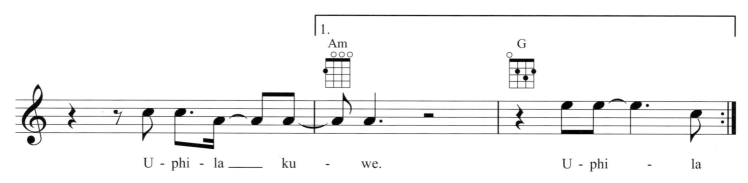

1.

U - phi - la _____ ku - we.   U - phi - la

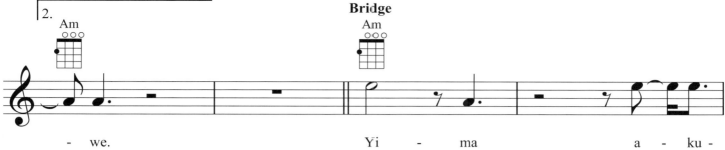

- we.   Yi - ma   a - ku -

na - bun - zi - ma. _____   Yi - va   la - ma - zwi ___ u - tha - le.

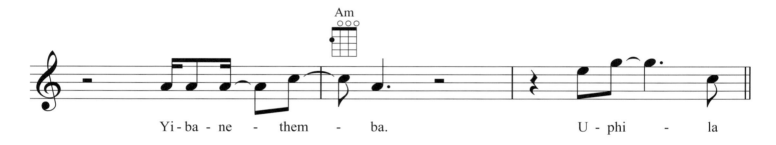

Yi - ba - ne - them - ba.   U - phi - la

Chorus

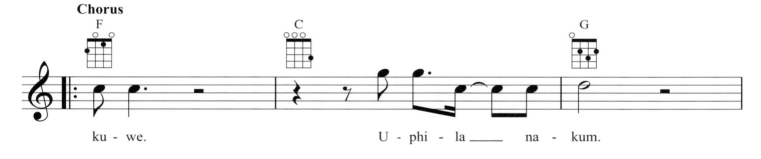

ku - we.   U - phi - la ___ na - kum.

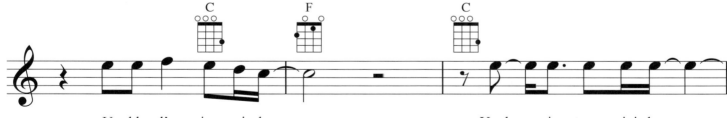

U - hla - l'e - jon - gi - le. _____   Yonk - in - to en - siyi - bo -

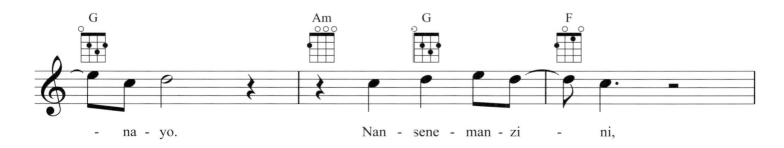

- na - yo.   Nan - sene - man - zi - ni,

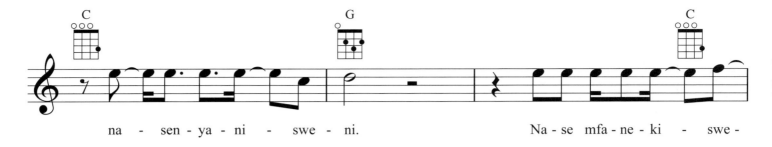

na - sen - ya - ni - swe - ni.   Na - se mfa - ne - ki - swe -

- ni wa - kho.   U - phi - la ___ ku - we.

U - phi - la   U - phi - la ___ ku - we.

English Translation

Here is a lion and a striped tiger.

Night and the spirit of life, calling. Listen.

And a voice, with the fear of a child, answers. Listen.

Throne of the ancestors.

Wait. There's no mountain too great.
Hear these words and have faith. Have faith.

Hey, listen.

He lives in you. He lives in me.
He watches over everything we see.
Into the water, into the truth,
In your reflection, he lives in you.
He lives in you.

Wait. There's no mountain too great.
Hear these words and have faith. Have faith.

He lives in you. He lives in me.
He watches over everything we see.
Into the water, into the truth,
In your reflection, he lives in you.
He lives in you.